*Dedicated to all those
who love to see
the Positive side of life*

NEW

REFLECTIONS

Gabrielle Kirby

Published by S.O.L. Productions Ltd.
Quarantine Hill, Wicklow Town,
Co. Wicklow, Ireland

Gabrielle Kirby asserts the moral right to be identified
as the author of this work.

ISBN 1-90171-225-7

Copyright © 2014 by Gabrielle Kirby

All rights reserved. No part of this publication may be
reproduced, stored in a retrieval system or transmitted in
any form or by any means, electronic, mechanical,
photocopying, recording or otherwise, without the prior,
written permission of the publisher.

All photographs by Gabrielle Kirby, except...
Pages 72, 78, 80, 112 - Seamus Byrne
Pages 13, 63 - Paul Diamond
Page 47 - Vincent Kirby
Page 56 - Shay Connolly
Graphic Design by Seamus Byrne

Printed in Ireland by
Conway Media

Dear Reader,

    'There's a crack in everything: that's how the light gets in'.

    Our brokenness is the beginning of our journey to health. Our mistakes are the springboards to amazing successes. Our failures and weaknesses, if used the right way, can give us extraordinary insights into the pursuit of happiness and peace and the things that really matter in life. Our only needed contribution to this amazing pattern of life is the constant admittance of who and what we are.

    To be inspired is a wonderful thing and I suppose all writers crave the moment when inspiration hits and they come out of the darkness into the light again.

    I suppose that would be my ideal: to inspire others so that 'seeds' can sprout, grow and flower.

    We are all so dependent on each other for encouragement, direction and inspiration.

Each story I've written started off as an inspiration in one form or another. I hope it will be an inspiration for you too.

Love,

Gabrielle

Contents

Introduction	5
Foreword	9
A Peaceful Nation	10
The Fire of Love	13
Goals	15
Plant a Seed	18
Use it or Lose it	20
Still Time	22
Always Another Chance	24
Every Breath We Take	26
A Wake-Up Call	28
Adventure	30
California	31
Don't Take Anything Personally	33
Have a Laugh	35
The Law of Forgiveness	38
Be Your Own Hero	40
You Are Loved	42
How Should We Pray?	44
When I Get Older	45
Peace	47
The Noose	50
The Beauty of Nature	52
Partridge Chicks	53
What You Do to Others	56
Does Age Matter?	58
Love Yourself	60
Loneliness	63

One Day at a Time	**66**
Risk Taking	**67**
The Better Part	**70**
Can't	**72**
Challenges	**74**
Change	**76**
Creating the World we Want	**78**
Times of Distress	**80**
Passing Through	**82**
'Angels'	**84**
Healing	**87**
Meditation	**88**
New York	**90**
Be in the Now	**92**
Opportunities	**94**
Responding to Inspirations	**96**
'Small'	**98**
What Would We Do?	**100**
'Wimp'	**102**
You Are A Unique Person	**104**
In Every Problem there's a Gift	**106**
Philomena	**108**
Programmes by Gabrielle Kirby	**112**
Healthy Holiday Retreats	**113**

Foreword

'She or he who walks by an inner light and is not unduly influenced by outward things needs no special time or place for prayers.

For the person of inner life is easily recollected, since they are never wholly immersed in outward affairs.

The person whose inner life is well-ordered and disposed is not troubled by the strange and perverse ways of others.

If your inner life were rightly ordered and your heart pure, all things would turn to your good and advantage'.

The Imitation of Christ by Thomas à Kempis

A PEACEFUL NATION

That two people remain at peace with one another for an extended length of time could be considered a miracle. For the inhabitants of a whole nation to be at peace 100% of the time could be considered a phenomenon! And, yet, this is the ideal we would like to hold on to, strive for and desire constantly.

For a nation to be at peace, we need each individual committed to striving for that goal. It requires a substantial contribution from each individual person. A starting point is 'Goodwill'. Goodwill towards the ideal. Goodwill and a belief that if we all make a little effort peace can and will be achieved.

Perhaps the first place to look might be within our own circle of close acquaintances, family or relatives. Are there people in that group whom we have ostracised for reasons we can hardly remember? Or maybe we are clinging to a conscious prejudice that we have allowed to harden our heart? If our words or actions are hostile, directly or indirectly, to these people, then we ourselves are living in a kind of mini 'war'.

An openness to peace means making room for that person or persons, trying to communicate with and understand them. It's really good to be as tolerant and forgiving as possible. And it's important to not speak badly about others. Ever. You know the old saying – 'If you haven't something good to say, don't say anything at all'.

We have to trust the goodness in ourselves and the goodness in others. Fear can place a big obstacle to this trust. Once fear gets a grip on our lives then we assume all manner of bad things are about to happen. It's not a written law, but 9 times out of 10, if you are kind to someone, they will be kind to you. But you can bet that if you are mean to someone, 10 times out of 10 they're going to retaliate negatively in some way.

Fear of the unknown can cause suspicion, doubt and insecurity. But when we face our fears we come to the realisation that a lot of fear is groundless, that in fact we don't have to act on our fears but rather trust in the inherent goodness in both ourselves and our neighbour. And how we deal with fear is important. Let's try to approach it with reason and care.

A man returned home one evening and heard a noise in his house. Assuming a burglary was taking place, he got his gun and shot the intruder he found in the wardrobe of his bedroom. It turned out to be his 10 year old daughter who was playing hide and seek with her friend. His daughter was supposed to be at a party elsewhere, but it was cancelled and she came home in time to play a game. Her last. Gripped by fear and a totally unfamiliar situation, the poor father was the cause of his daughter's death.

Finally, we need to learn to forgive ourselves, learn from our mistakes and live with peace in our hearts. If I don't like myself, how am I going to like someone else? From within my peaceful heart I build bridges of peace to the members of my family, my friends and then to people of other races, creeds and colours.

The nation's peace very much begins with me.

TIP TO GO:
Get rid of the clutter in your mind, body and spirit. The simple things in life can be a great aid to peace.

THE FIRE OF LOVE

Fire is fuelled by what you throw onto it. It burns brighter because of the purity of the fuel and to keep the fire burning brightly, you need a constant supply of the very best fuel.

There is no 'best' fuel for the Fire of Love. It takes every offering it receives, no matter what it is. The only requirement for the fuel is that it is freely given. For example, you get hurt, either physically or emotionally and you are in pain, extreme pain. What are your choices at this point?

- Try to get revenge.
- Become bitter and increase your pain
- Throw all your pain on the Fire of Love.

By throwing your pain on the Fire of Love you are making a huge contribution to a mystical pool of love that can be used for good in the world. In fact, you don't know how it will be used, but once you cast all your pain onto the fire, to a certain extent you free yourself from the burden of it, and if you repeatedly do this with all the pain in your everyday life, you strengthen your resolve to only live by love.

The Fire of Love accepts all offerings, no matter how insignificant they may appear to be, from the smallest pinprick to the greatest catastrophe; every single item of dislike, disturbance, annoyance of any kind, hurt, disappointment, sickness. The list is endless, but all are welcome.

The 'fire' needs to burn brightly. Keep the fire alight with your contributions big and small and watch how your world changes for the better. And you will experience a new growth in wisdom, understanding and compassion.

TIP TO GO:
What can you throw on the fire of love to keep it constantly burning bright?
Keep a watchful eye on your inner world.
Make the best use of every situation.

GOALS

What goals do you have? Do you have a life goal? A weekly goal? Even a daily goal? If you want to be motivated, you need to have a goal. Highly motivated people are people with goals. They set goals for themselves all the time. Having a goal supplies you with an enormous amount of energy. Goals are part of the indomitable human spirit. Having a goal can raise your spirits, supply you with positive visions of what you can achieve if you apply yourself to any given situation, no matter how fantastic it may seem to you. Having a goal and trying to achieve it is your ticket to happiness, peace, harmony and, most of all, fulfilment.

The first priority is goal setting. This requires silent time reflecting on what you want. What do you really want to do with your life? What unique contribution can you make to the world? What talents do you need to achieve your goals? The first thing to consider is the fact that you are unique. You are a unique human being with talents, desires and passions. It doesn't matter what you decide to do, even if it's out there already; you are going to do it in a remarkable way because you are different. You are unique.

The next important point is to be positive about your goals. Ideas will emerge as you reflect. Write down all your ideas, especially whatever fills you with enthusiasm. At this point, you may not know which way to go, but seeing your goals written down will give you ideas what direction to take.

You can have several major goals. Your long-term goals could be between 3 - 4 years and your short term goals could be between 3 - 4 months. When you program a goal into your mind, everything in you goes about trying to make it happen. There is great power in goal-setting. As you go with the flow of life and strive for your goals, something will emerge that you want to do more than anything else. You may have several things you want to achieve. Go at them all for the moment and see where they take you.

It's important to encourage yourself, to reflect on the goal, on the end product, and try to be the best you can be. There will be times when you may forget about your goal, get involved in the humdrum of life, but because you need fulfilment to be happy, you will eventually return to your goal again. Don't worry about lost time – weeks, months, years even. You can take up your heart's desire at any time. The important thing is not to die with the music of your life still unattempted.

Don't wait. Do it now. Do some little thing in relation to your goal. Make a list. Pray. Practice your singing - whatever it is. Do it. Don't worry about failure. Failure is only postponed success.

Goals can completely change the direction of your life. But one thing's for sure, once you set goals for yourself you can nearly sit back and watch them being accomplished before your very eyes.

George emerged from a goal-setting seminar with the goal of having a better relationship with his son. A year later he wrote to the man in charge to thank him for changing his life. He had spent much needed quality-time with his 8 year old son, who had been killed in a recent accident. Although George was grief-stricken, he felt no guilt. He had achieved his goal.

TIP TO GO:
Don't wait.
Single out your goals for today. See the difference it can make to your life. Good Luck!

PLANT A SEED

So often, we don't do what we want to do. We make excuses for not carrying out things close to our heart, and then, because we have failed, we feel bad about ourselves and become terribly self-critical, even hating ourselves.

When you get an inspiration, no matter how small it is – go for it. You are planting a seed that will come to fruition. You are beginning something that will be a part of giving yourself and giving love; and no matter how little that love is, it will bear fruit, both in this world and in the next.

Planting a seed is making a new beginning. And you can have new beginnings every day. Because God is good, He showers us with inspirations. We only have to open our hearts and allow Him to come in.

Open your heart and plant a seed. A seed of happiness, peace, love, humour, caring, forgiveness. The list is endless.

Planting a seed is probably the most positive thing you can do for yourself and for others. To plant a seed is to look up with new hope for better things. It is to believe that love has the power to conquer all obstacles, overcome all ills and make the rough paths smooth. You may not be there when the 'fruit' arrives, but it doesn't matter. You have spread happiness, love and encouragement to so many on the journey of life, who all need a helping hand to reach the heights of their potential.

>Never fail to plant a seed.

TIP TO GO:
Become more grounded.
Work in your garden.
Walk in the woods.

USE IT OR LOSE IT

Cosmonauts returning from Soyuz 34 space flight had to be taken off the spacecraft on stretchers because, after 175 days in space, their muscles and bones had deteriorated to the point where they were unable to stand. Their legs would not support them. Why? Not enough stress was put on their muscles or bones to warrant their use during space flight. Interesting! What we don't use will not support us in time of need.

It seems to be a lot like faith. No use waiting until the calamity happens to draw on our faith, because it may not be there. We need to use it every day, in all circumstances, so there is a well to draw from in time of need. As the saying goes, 'Use it or lose it!' Just as the astronauts lost the use of their muscles and bones, we run the risk of losing our wisdom and insight if we don't acknowledge and use them every day. This could be the root cause of much increased anxiety, worry and stress in our society.

Faith adds a light touch to our lives. It gives us a comic view of ourselves and the situations we get into. It helps us know the important things in life, what really matters, and to let go of the less important. It helps us see the 'big picture'.

We are completely in charge of how much faith we have stored up. It's a choice. It may be given to us as the smallest of seeds, but it has the possibility of becoming something big and useful in our life, if we want it to be.

Astronauts take a giant step for mankind. Why not try a leap of faith for yourself?

TIP TO GO:
Test out your faith in different situations.
Take a risk.
Be adventurous.
Let go and let God.

STILL TIME

Silence. How wonderful that can be. To lie down, stretch out fully and be still. To be healthy in mind, body and spirit we need to be in the presence of silence at least once a day.

Silence is the beginning of contemplation. Allow the silence to continue, allow all thoughts to float away, not holding on to a single one. Let go of everything. This time is for you and God.

The presence of God is around us constantly, in nature, in our loved ones, in every little thing that goes on in our lives. God is there. But He may be on the outside. Being still puts us in touch with Him immediately. Brings us closer to Him. But it's our choice to invite Him in.

TIP TO GO:
Create a silent moment.
It's a wonderful time for healing, rejuvenation and peace.

ALWAYS ANOTHER CHANCE

Mary was 14. She could never see eye to eye with her mother. She felt her mother was too hard on her, always picking on her and asking where she was going. It annoyed her no end. They fought continually. But there were times when they were the best of friends. At those times, she liked it when her mother was more of a friend than someone always telling her what to do.

One day, her mother wanted some insignificant thing done, but Mary didn't want to do it. She was in a hurry to meet her friends. They fought and words best left unsaid passed between them. Mary stormed out, vowing not to come back anytime soon.

That evening, as Mary strolled home along the street, she thought about what was ahead of her. There and then she made up her mind to apologise. She never got the chance. Her mother had died of a heart attack while she was gone.

Mary is 24 now, married with children of her own. She regrets to this day the fight she had with her mother and, not so much the fight, but the fact that she never had the opportunity to say how sorry she was.

She has that chance now with her own chidren.

TIP TO GO:
Give your mother a break.
Plan a day together every once in a while.
Decide not to argue for 24hrs.
Try to love her the way she is. After all, she was once a young person just like you.

EVERY BREATH WE TAKE

'Every breath you take, every move you make, I'll be watching you.'

These lines from a famous song always remind me of God, because, even though we may not be aware of it, God is watching us. Just as the lines from the song are from a loved one to his beloved, so too is God watching us out of love. Not criticising nor condemning us in any way, but just simply loving us.

God loves every breath we take and move we make towards loving Him.

TIP TO GO:
Take time out to communicate with God, or just sit in silence and allow Him to fill you with His love.

A WAKE-UP CALL

A friend of mine got a 'wake-up call'. He had a heart attack. He knew his life was full of stress and his diet appalling. He had been to health farms several times, so he knew the right and wrong of his dietary needs. But he continued to spiral downwards until he was just barely able to dial 999.

Now back on track, he feels lucky to have got another chance. But how long will it last? He tells me the reason he got into that state in the first place was because of loneliness.

Loneliness is hard to combat. Perhaps we need to return to our roots - to build communities where people care about each other; where entertainment means inviting friends over for a meal, a chat, some story-telling and good fun.

In this stress-filled world we all need playtime. We need to rid ourselves of the burdens of the day through laughter, dance and all sorts of creative pursuits. Instead of resorting to pills, perhaps we could dance away the blues, sing into a hairbrush or something 'mad' like that which takes us away from the things that bring us down and cause us to be obsessed with ourself and our lot.

Unfortunately, we cannot overcome loneliness for somebody else. But each of us has a need to communicate with another person, to stop thinking about oneself long enough to know that there are other people around who need caring for, looking after and interest shown them.

If you're lonely, perhaps it's a call to go visit a neighbour, to be there for a friend. It could be a call from the depths of yourself to be fulfilled through following your heart's desire. Going back to your roots can give you that, can show you the right direction to head in.

You're never too old to discover the treasure within yourself, your inherent potential to reach out and brighten up the lives of others, and, in the process, free yourself from the terrible plague of loneliness.

TIP TO GO:
Be on the lookout for ways to fulfil your heart's desire.
Use your talents for the benefit of yourself and others.

Kids know how to play!

ADVENTURE

The word *adventure* conjures up visions of bungee jumping, safari, bathing in tropical waters. But the most important time to be adventurous may be in your everyday life - greeting people you don't like, inviting a neighbour to dinner, overcoming a grudge...

TIP TO GO:
Let go of the past.
Make room for adventure.
Give away something.

CALIFORNIA

Taking a trip to California on my own some time ago was a daunting experience. My fear of flying revolves mostly around taking off. I'm not actually hit with it until the plane is lifting up. Landing takes care of itself as I'm inclined to think if we've come this far nothing can go wrong!

I sat beside a man who immediately struck up a conversation with me and continued to engage me in conversation so much that we were actually in the air before I knew it – what a blessing! It says a lot for being distracted and involved in doing something other than concentrating on what you're afraid of.

Fear is an extraordinary thing. We're afraid of so many things, one of them being 'what others think'. Who are those 'others' and why do we care so much what 'they' think? If the truth be told, there are no 'others' and 'they' don't exist. We're presented with something we want to do or achieve and fear comes along trying to prevent us from realising our goal. Fear is only hot air. Speak your fear and you're presented with ways to overcome it. That fearful challenge, when broken down, is made manageable. One step at a time, one moment at a time is all it takes.

Touchdown in New York. Then, on to California. What a fantastic holiday! Each plane journey a new, exciting situation - to be FEARED? I don't think so. Just handled as the problem arose, if you'll excuse the pun.

TIP TO GO:
Prepare for the unexpected while travelling.
Bring a cushion, a game, some dried fruit.
Anything that could add to your enjoyment of the journey.

DON'T TAKE ANYTHING PERSONALLY

You know, one of the hardest things to do is not to take things personally. When somebody, usually a friend, says something that cuts you to the quick, your first inclination is to take it personally and hit back with an equally smart or curt remark.

We have to try and realise that when somebody says or does something hurtful, the problem is with them and not us. Even though they may vent how they feel on us, it is still nothing to do with us.

It takes time to wise-up and realise that perhaps your friend is just looking for encouragement, sympathy or a helping hand. Their search for help is just cloaked in hurting others, specifically you, because you happen to be the closest to them.

Even though it may be personal, only the small-minded person takes things personally. The big-minded, big–hearted person sees beyond the remark, realises that the person who has hurt them just simply has their own problems.

The Inuit Eskimos, when something hurtful or dangerous happened to their young children, would take them in their arms and rock them back and forth while laughing. Their purpose was to keep open the lines of clear thought so that if and when they got into difficult situations, laughter would keep their minds clear, thereby showing them ways of escaping their forthcoming dilemma, perhaps even saving their lives.

There's always something profitable to learn when we get hurt. There's always a change to be made, a tie to be severed or a friendship to be mended. You decide. Don't get stuck inside yourself. Look out and see what lesson there is to learn.

TIP TO GO:
Be really kind to yourself when you get hurt.
Go out and celebrate, with a friend if you can, by having a favourite dessert. Treat yourself in some way and try not to think about the hurt.
Rent out a comedy movie. Sometimes laughter gives you a proper perspective on the situation.

I ASKED THE LORD TO BLESS YOU
IN SUCH A SPECIAL WAY.
THAT YOU WILL KNOW WITHIN YOUR HEART
THAT SOMEONE PRAYED FOR YOU TODAY.

I ASKED GOD GRANT YOU STRENGTH AND HAPPINESS
AND A SPECIAL ANSWER TO YOUR PRAYER.
TO WRAP YOU IN HIS ARMS WITH HIS
PROTECTING CARE.

I ASKED THAT HE FILL EACH DAY AHEAD OF YOU
WITH BLESSINGS FROM ABOVE.
SO THAT YOU WILL KNOW TODAY AND ALWAYS
THE FULLNESS OF HIS LOVE.

HAVE A LAUGH

What a great gift it is to have a sense of humour. How freeing it is to have a good laugh. The benefits are innumerable. Laughing boosts your immune system, makes you feel good about yourself and makes life worth living again, especially when you're going through a bad patch. But what gives you the ability to laugh at a situation, to see the comical side of failure, to get some respite from the humdrum business of earning a living and trying to make ends meet?

I think believing that good will conquer evil plays a big part, and, if that's the case, then there isn't so much to worry about. The worries of the world need not be on our shoulders, because God can bring good out of any situation, no matter how bad it is. He is in charge. Because He is in charge you can feel safe. Bad things may happen, but good things will happen too. We need to make the choice to only be interested in the things that make us feel good and make life worth living.

It is our choice to lighten up when things seem impossible. To leave worry aside, sending good thoughts out into the world for the benefit of others. To lighten the daily load of our fellow human beings by greeting them with a smile and thinking positively about them.

Sensible, healthy choices will help keep you

stress-free and on top of every situation. Always leave time for the unexpected, especially where children are concerned. Don't leave everything to the last minute, otherwise you will be stressed out and in a panic at a time when you need to be in control. We cause ourselves a lot of stress when we refuse to slow down. When you feel in a panic, take time out for a minute or two, breathe deeply and recollect your thoughts. Move slowly and deliberately. A few minutes can make a huge difference to your equilibrium and just give you the edge that you need. If you have the presence of mind, you can even induce a laugh by doing or saying something extremely silly, just anything to cut through the seriousness of the moment and bring on a laugh. Laughter can dissolve much tension and pressure, leaving you clear-headed and ready for action.

TIP TO GO:
To Induce a laugh...
Grab hold of your tummy with both hands. For the person who has a little extra weight here this will be a piece of cake! Shake your tummy up and down. At the same time shout 'Ha! Ha! Ha!' The louder the better. This usually has the effect of making you laugh. The very fact of doing something ridiculous can cause you to feel silly, thereby making you laugh even more, which is the objective. Do this until the laughter takes a hold. Try this any time you feel you are taking life too seriously.

THE LAW OF FORGIVENESS

You are mentally healthy to the degree that you can forgive and forget grievances against you. Your willingness to forgive others and let go of past grievances is the single most important determinant in whether or not you are a fully integrated, fully functioning human being – so says the law of forgiveness.

What makes it really difficult to forgive at times is the fact that we want to believe that the hurt we experienced at the hand of the person who caused it was deliberate in one way or another; that the person who hurt me doesn't like me, or their esteem for me isn't very high.

Whether it's true or not doesn't really matter, but forgiving them does. The person who suffers most from not forgiving is you. You will be the one who will suffer, because your mind will be taken up with the deed that has been done against you and you won't be able to let go. Being caught up with past deeds will keep you in the past and won't allow you to move on. The place to be at all times is in the present moment.

That's what life is - full of exciting moments for you to create, to love, to be what you want to be, what God wants you to be. There are only so many minutes in each day to do all that you have to do. Why waste any of it getting caught up with the past? The past is dead and gone. Let go and give yourself a life. If you want to be full of life, drop the past, even if it's only an hour ago. Holding on leaves you behind.

Life is too exciting to waste, even for a second.

TIP TO GO:
Is there a person you find hard to forgive?
Wish them well.
Send them a blessing.
Think good thoughts about them.
Say a little prayer for them.
Write them a letter explaining how you feel about the situation; tell them you forgive them; seal the letter; you don't have to send it - just dispose of it. You have forgiven them.

BE YOUR OWN HERO

We often set standards for ourselves that we just cannot live up to and although it's an excellent idea to have high ideals and to always aim for the summit, nevertheless there are times when being your own hero is the most sensible and encouraging thing you can do for yourself.

Be your own hero, march to your own drum, go at your own pace. Just be really happy being who you are - yourself. Who can really tell you what you should be? After all, when you open yourself to your own wisdom, listen in silence to your own inner voice, can you not then make ground-breaking decisions to become the person only you know how to be?

Being your own hero means drawing encouragement from everything you put your mind to. Every effort is a success. Comparisons are unnecessary, guilt unheard of. Every enterprise undertaken will just be a succession of positive efforts in the total enjoyment of who you are, on every single day that has been given to you.

TIP TO GO:
Shed what is not 'you'.
Love who you are.

'I'm a Hero'

YOU ARE LOVED

You are on a journey. Your only companion is God. He goes every place you go. Everything you go through, you go through with Him. He is your guide. You slip. Fall. Get hurt. Are disappointed. He is there to provide for all your needs. He has a vast store of love that supplies every single thing you need for your journey. If you can keep going on the journey and don't give up, bliss and peace will be your reward. Even in this life, you will always see light at the end of the tunnel.

See the work of His Hand behind every single thing that goes on in your life. Nothing, not one thing, happens by accident. God is involved in it all, and not just involved, but waiting by your side with out-stretched hand for you to take, freely, when you are ready. He is there without in any way pressuring you, kindly keeping a distance. Just waiting.

TIP TO GO:
Call Him sometime.

HOW SHOULD WE PRAY?

Formal prayer can mean little or nothing, but when prayer is viewed in the light of love, everything changes. When you look at a person with love, you are praying. When you laugh with another, you are praying. When you cry with a friend because of some mishap, you are praying. Prayer takes many forms. We just have to find the one that suits us. Christ said, 'Where there are two or more gathered in my name, there I am in the midst of them.'

TIP TO GO:
God is in charge of all things, big and small.
Have confidence in Him.
Worry not.

WHEN I GET OLDER

What a sad day it is when there's no other option but to put your ageing parent into a home. Your parent has reached a stage where they need care 24 hours a day, and you're not able to provide it. They can't remember who you are, so are frightened every time you appear on the scene. They upbraid you for not dropping by, even though you are there for them as much as you can. They can't remember things they've done extremely well for years - how to cook, make a cup of tea, dress themselves. You are torn between wanting to do everything for them or allowing professional caregivers to take over.

When I visit my mother in her new 'home', she talks about the house she's living in as her 'new house' and the people she's surrounded by as her 'visitors'. She has so much work to do looking after them, she hardly has a minute to herself!

Although she seems to recognise my face and is happy to see me, she doesn't really know who I am. All the love she has for me is trapped inside her and cannot get out. A friend, offering an explanation of her condition said to me, 'She's in heaven already'. That's a consoling thought. A wonderful woman who tirelessly worked all her life for her children is already reaping her reward by being looked after 24 hours a day, 7 days a week and, on top of that, she has the whole host of heaven waiting to welcome her into her mansion.

TIP TO GO:
Treasure the time you have with your parents.
Let them know how much you love them.

PEACE

Yes, we all love a bit of peace and quiet and we can probably remember when that's all our parents wanted at times - just a little peace and quiet! We need peace to restore our sense of balance and harmony. Without it, we are out of sync. But how do we get peace on a grand scale? How do we restore peace to people who've been at war for aeons?

I think the place to begin is at home. By 'home' I mean within one's heart. We need peace first and foremost in our own heart. It is from there peace radiates outward, to our family, friends, neighbours and out to the world at large.

Peace comes from the high value or appreciation we put on each present moment and the realisation that what we do in the moment adds to or subtracts from the well-being of the world. We have to look into our hearts and see if we are building or destroying. One good guideline is - being positive builds, being negative destroys. Being positive helps us to be open to new ideas, cultures and peoples. If we have problems with what is new or unfamiliar, being positive helps us dialogue with others so as to arrive at a solution that is good for all.

Peace also comes as a result of personal discipline. Even though we may not like the sound of the word or what it entails, it remains true when tried and tested. To hold back an angry word, a smart remark or a caustic glare makes a huge contribution to peace. It may seem very small, but little acts of kindness have huge power and really make a difference. If we all care for each other and discipline ourselves so as to curb our natural self-interest and try to think of what is good for everyone, serious conflict is unlikely in such a atmosphere.

Historically, there are many ordinary human beings, people just like you and I, who have brought about extraordinary change by peaceful means. Mahatma Gandhi, Nelson Mandela, Martin Luther King and Rosa Parks to mention but a few. Rosa Parks, just an ordinary black woman in the Southern States of the USA, decided she was tired standing up in the city bus, and when she sat down, and thereby broke 'white-rule', the whole world began to change around her. All she wanted was a little peace and quiet.

Why wait around for peace to come about? Nothing happens unless you make it happen. No matter who you are or what walk of life you're in you can make a difference. You don't have to think, 'If I was in power, this is what I would do'. You are in power! You are in control of the most important person on the planet - yourself. Begin with peace in your own heart and from there allow your unique contribution to develop. The world wants and needs you and your social offering, so don't be afraid. We are all waiting for what you have to give.

The Chinese proverb says, 'A journey of a

thousand miles begins with one step'. Make that first step now!

TIP TO GO:
Contribute to world peace by being kind to someone who annoys and irritates you.
Choose to only see goodness.
Send a prayer out into the World.

THE NOOSE

We have a tendency at times to make rash judgements about ourselves and our neighbours. Have we any idea of the noose we tie around our neck when we get involved in the activity of judging? Not only do we restrict the freedom of our neighbour, but we put an end to our own freedom. It certainly comes easy to judge, but the consequences are huge. Every time we judge rashly we lose a little bit of our personal freedom.

Kind judgements set the tone for a happy environment and liberate the atmosphere for creative endeavours.

Christ's directive is insightful and simple – 'Judge not and you shall not be judged.'

The only judgement that is really acceptable is kind judgement. Better to err on the side of being too kind than too harsh. Kind judgement makes for personal peace. Then, when we are at peace with ourselves, that peace is extended to our neighbour. And many neighbours at peace makes for a peaceful world.

Jane was tired and went into a city cafe for a cup of coffee and some biscuits. The only seat available was beside an African man. She settled down and began to drink her coffee. The man leaned over and took a biscuit from the packet on the plate. Jane was appalled. She said nothing and had one herself. After a few minutes, the man leaned over again and took another. Jane was infuriated and sharply said, 'Where I come from we ask before we take something that's not ours! The man looked at her and said nothing. Jane finished her coffee and left.

On the bus home, she reached into her bag to take out a book and discovered the packet of biscuits she had bought in the cafe. Unopened.

The African gentleman had been eating his own biscuits.

TIP TO GO:
Put a good motive on the actions of others.

THE BEAUTY OF NATURE

The beauty of nature is there for all to see, but not everyone is in a position to appreciate it. Sometimes it's necessary to focus in on it, be it a flower, an insect or just water gently flowing by, to really come to know it, appreciate it and allow it to have an effect on you.

Nature is one way to experience God's beauty.

TIP TO GO:
Look with love and appreciation at creation.
Inhale it's revelations.

PARTRIDGE CHICKS

Some time ago, I travelled to a Health Centre in the USA. I wanted to fast for several days in an effort to improve my health.

The centre is situated on beautiful grounds, surrounded by weeping willows and exotic shrubs of many kinds. This magnificent garden rests in the creative hands of Brendan, a gardener who performs his labour of love several times a week. Not only is he a wonderful gardener, but he has a wealth of knowledge about absolutely everything that happens in his domain. His singular delight, the time I was there, was showing me an enormous cactus that only flowers once every hundred years, and this year was that important year! From the centre of the cactus a stem had shot up 30ft into the air, from which a flower would blossom and last all but 24 hours before falling off, showering its seeds onto the ground to eventually create hundreds of new cacti. Brendan wanted to be around for that sighting.

Brendan also knew every creature that came and went, where they came from and how long they would be around. He let me in on a secret - there was a family of partridges living close by. But he thought it highly unlikely anyone might see them because they are such a shy bird. And especially when they have young, they are even more cautious. I suppose they resemble the cactus somewhat, inclined only to show their beauty to God. If they came out at all, it might only be when the sun was going down, because that's the time that's most quiet and all the patients are watching television. I thought, 'How nice it would be to see this little family of unusual birds.'

Feeling nauseated (due to my detoxing fast) and not able to watch television, I sat out in the warm, evening garden for a few quiet moments on my reclining chair, breathing in pure country air, hoping for my weak state to pass. From behind, I heard a faint fluttering of wings. Too weak to turn around and look, I lay completely still. Another flutter! Another and another and another - like a fluttering of angel wings gathering around me! In my delighted stillness I found myself surrounded on all sides by partridge chicks - eleven of them! I was afraid to even breathe or take a glance in case I might frighten them, but they came closer and closer. Perhaps they sensed my weakened fasting state and, in compassion, were inviting me to their family mealtime…

I gazed, not moving, with sheer delight, mesmerised. Eleven of the most beautiful Partridge chicks, guided by mother and father, picking all around me in a perfect circle. For me, a moment of utter beauty. For Brendan, a story I could not wait to tell!

TIP TO GO:
Loving our experiences of weakness opens us to many experiences of beauty.

WHAT YOU DO TO OTHERS

I saw a film recently about a young man who was murdered. His mother was inconsolable and set out on a path of vengeance to make sure the murderer suffered for all the pain and hurt he had caused her family. She infected her entire family with the same hate she experienced.

Her hatred dogged her life. Not able to sleep at night, she took medication for insomnia. She frequently coughed up blood from bleeding ulcers caused by the stress of her hatred. She attended each parole meeting of the now model prisoner and vented her rage on the parole board to make sure the prisoner never got out of prison.

Her friends were worried about her as her health spiralled downward. They suggested she meet with the prisoner and talk with him. The meeting was a disaster; she couldn't control her anger and rage at the young man from the second she met him. Amazingly, she continued to meet with him. At each subsequent meeting she became less and less angry. She began to experience the human being behind the murderer. She was able to sleep at night without medication and her ulcers calmed down.

At the next parole meeting, she spoke about the wrong he had done, but she also spoke about the importance of getting another chance in life. He was let out on parole. She discovered that by giving him another chance at life, she had equally given herself another chance.

The power of forgiveness had restored health, not only to her body, but to her mind and spirit too. What you do to others, you do to yourself.

TIP TO GO:
Negative thoughts rob you of your peace of mind. Nip them in the bud as soon as they appear.

DOES AGE MATTER?

Are there any advantages to being old?' a friend of mine is always asking. He seems to find it an unnerving experience even though he's not that old, nor is he incapacitated in any way. He just finds the thought of 'getting old' an unpleasant prospect.

What do I say to him? 'You're not old', or 'Don't look on yourself as old', when in fact the truth is we are getting older by the minute. But I think every age has its own unique beauty.

When I was 25 years old, I thought there couldn't be anything interesting after the age of 30. Now that I'm way on the other side of 30, I find life fascinating. Age is relative really; it just depends on what you want to do with your life, what direction you want it to take and, more importantly, how positive your outlook is.

I remember I attended a meeting with my mother some time ago. In the course of the evening we got separated. I was talking to a middle-aged man who pointed out a friend of his to me saying, 'She's just beside that old woman over there'. When I looked in the direction he was pointing, I was appalled. He had just referred to my mother as 'an old woman'.

When you regard another person with love or have a relationship that is encouraging, enriching and uplifting, how could age possibly enter the picture?

Surely that would be an insult to love?

My mother, whom I regarded as a wonderful friend, was now 'an old woman' to a stranger. But, I suppose, that's the reality of life.

However, maybe sometimes it's better to live in an unreal world, a world more conducive to the priorities of love, caring and meaningful relationships.

TIP TO GO:
Develop a positive attitude, no matter what age you are.
Wonderful experiences can be yours at any age.
Quality of life matters more than a long life.

LOVE YOURSELF

The directive to 'Love your neighbour as yourself' is fine. But what if you don't love yourself? How are you ever going to love your neighbour?

Why is it such a difficult task to love yourself? Why do we shy away from loving ourselves? Of course, you may say, what is there to love anyway?

The very first step in loving yourself is to realise you are a unique human being, created out of love, for love. You are like nobody else; there is not another person like you in the entire world. Your potential is endless. You have a unique contribution to make to the world and you cannot realise your potential without first of all recognising this uniqueness and all of its implications.

The second step in loving yourself is to positively attack all your weak areas. What do you hate or dislike most about yourself? What is your predominant weakness and how much pain does it cause in your life? Make a list, if you have to, and set about giving yourself a positive solution to each thing you dislike in yourself. Having a weakness is not the end of the world. In fact, it means you have the potential to develop a strength opposite to that weakness. Instead of being depressed because of your weaknesses, they become a source of self-confidence.

Begin by trying to find something good in each

flaw or weakness you find in yourself. For example, you might have a feature you dislike. Every time your attention is drawn to this feature, find something good in it. Say to yourself, for example, 'I love the way my teeth are crooked', or 'I love that my hair is straight,' or whatever it happens to be. The more you compliment yourself on what you hate about yourself, the more you open up to seeing how unique it makes you. The more you love the flaw and, through it, love yourself, the more you will be set free from yourself. Then you will be able to enjoy yourself, as well as love and enjoy the beauty of your neighbour.

Loving yourself is not something that is accomplished in a day or a month. It's a constant effort to supply yourself with positive thoughts, because within each of us is a negative critic. The negative critic likes to highlight our weak points, areas where we know we constantly fail. But we can instantly recognise this critic, if we are on our guard and ready to supply the positive each time an opportunity arises.

Developing a loving attitude toward ourselves is just good sense. We need to let ourselves off the hook for not being perfect, throw ourselves a bone, be prepared to forgive and forget.

Part of loving yourself is not to deride yourself when you fail. Try to see the good side of every situation, whether it be a transgression, a failure or just giving into a weakness. Learn to have compassion on yourself. And, of course, the more perfectly you love yourself, the more love you will have for your neighbour.

Because you love yourself and everything about yourself, you set yourself free. Free to enjoy and be interested in everything and everyone around you.

Make the love of yourself your first priority. Not only will you reap the benefits, but your neighbour will too!

TIP TO GO:
Write out 10 things you love about yourself.

LONELINESS

Loneliness seems to be a huge problem in our world today. Why is that? One would think, with all our technological advancements, that we would be able to make contact with someone when we are feeling lonely. There are so many wonderful things going on everywhere that you would think it easy to get involved, to reach out to someone and have a heart-to-heart conversation; just to share how you are feeling, what you think about things of importance, and just to have some fun with another human being.

If you join Facebook, you immediately seem to have a thousand friends. People you don't even know latch on to your page and, although it can be fun and very interesting, it is still no substitute for the real thing: a human being whom you can talk to about what is going on in your life, your hopes, your dreams and the contribution you would like to make for this world to be a better place.

Most people, without realising it, need something a bit deeper than acquiring a thousand friends overnight. Sometimes we need just one person to give us a few minutes, to listen to what we have to say. It's easy to post things on the internet and it's a wonderful tool, yet it cannot be a substitute for real human contact where you can look into the eyes of another human being while you are talking to them, make a connection and share a moment of joy together; where you know if you have said too little or too much by the way the other person reacts to you.

There is just no substitute for having a friend. Everyone, no matter who they are, needs a friend. St Brigid, the 6th century Irish saint, declared that the person without a friend was like a body without a head. We are not sufficient on our own. We were not created to be on our own. Sometimes our thoughts are too much for us. We need to bounce them off others to see what the real truth is. We are intrinsically attached to other people. We need them and they need us, and the more we come to this truthful realisation, the better chance we have of happiness and peace of mind. We need to love and be loved and the quickest way to be loved is to love others. It's hard to get away from the old maxims... 'Give and you will receive', 'Love begets love', 'Kindness begets kindness', and on it goes.

A terrific movement that has been going around for a while is 'Pay it Forward'. It really just means sharing some of the joy in your life with other human beings by doing something for them without them necessarily knowing about it. It can be your contribution to making the world a much better place. When you make it good for somebody else, you are making it good for yourself. Never let a day pass without doing something good for your neighbour, especially the neighbour you may not feel like doing something for. Why? Because everybody is lonely sometimes and you might be the very person to make a big difference in their life.

TIP TO GO:
Share your thoughts with another human being.

ONE DAY AT A TIME

The prisoner protested against his sentence.

'I just can't do 10 years, judge!' he pleaded.
'Can you do one day?' questioned the judge.
'Oh yes!' replied the prisoner.
'Well, do 10 years, one day at a time.'

The easy way through any difficult situation no matter what form it takes - pain, job loss, relationship problems or just inclement weather - is to take it one day at a time. Better still, when difficulties seem insurmountable, go through them one moment at a time.

TIP TO GO:
There are times when we may feel imprisoned by a chosen lifestyle, workload or just plain stress. Take a day off just for yourself to relax, enjoy and get your priorities right.

RISK TAKING

Risk taking always demands courage. To go it alone is not easy, but when done can be extremely rewarding. You have taken an unmarked trail. You have asserted your right to be free, taken the road your inner voice is inspiring you to take. You are nervous as you set out; fears lurk in the background, but your enthusiasm for this new venture fills your mind, body and spirit. You are ready to ascend to new heights, never taken before. You don't know what's over the hill, but you are on your way up and ready for anything.

Every new venture undertaken challenges your comfort zone. It demands that you take life in the moment and live it to the full. When you throw caution to the wind you find new security and confidence in yourself that you didn't already have, but always hoped was there.

Risk taking is what children do every day, hundreds of times a day, as they grow up. Their life is one of exploration, finding out, doing what they've never done before and, a lot of time, receiving a fair amount of criticism for what they do. Still, they carry on pushing back their horizons. It's how they grow.

To return to that state of simplicity and childlikeness involves taking risks, perhaps attempting one thing you are afraid of every day, perhaps doing something you've never done before but always wanted to do. By facing these challenges head on, you are establishing a new state of freedom in yourself.

As Jenny's mother was coming out of her local supermarket, she happened to see her daughter, barely 14, hanging out with one of the weirdest guys imaginable. He had studs all over his face and rings in his lips. At home, she pondered her best approach to the situation. When Jenny eventually came home, she approached her saying: 'Why don't you bring your boyfriends home instead of just hanging around the street?' Jenny did just that. This way, she knew where her daughter was and, besides, discovered that even though a person may look a little weird, they can be the nicest person in the world.

When parents don't approve of their children's friends, they add mystery to attraction and a desire in their children to defy them. Loving your child is also loving who they love or, at least, if you can't love their friends, you can try to see the good side of the choices they've made - it's a confidence boost for your children and one they will really appreciate in the long run.

TIP TO GO:
Live each day to the full.
Enjoy yourself.
Enjoy your life.

THE BETTER PART

We want the best for ourselves. Always. When we hear there's something better available, no matter what area it's in, we automatically want it. We want good things for ourselves, our children, family, friends and for all peoples in the world. We also want the best for the environment. We have an inherent need to take care of what has been given to us, to play a part in preserving the goodness and beauty of the natural world. It's why we take time to recycle, support the growing and buying of organically-grown produce, cottage industries, etc. We always choose the better option every time, provided we are free to do so.

When it comes to what we really need or want deep down, we are sometimes inclined to take what comes and not fight for our deeper spiritual needs. Prolonged bouts of pressure call for relaxation time, and offers of relaxing weekends and meditation classes often come our way and we think, 'Oh I would love that! I could really do with that.' But we immediately put it on the long finger, way out of reach, instead of making a commitment there and then. Okay, maybe we couldn't possibly afford the time or money for a weekend, but we could arrange an hour out of our day to meditate and relax. Where there's a will there's a way. We just need to hold the thought and apply it when we have the time, or rather, when we choose to make the time.

A quiet hour of relaxation/meditation, once a day, or even once a week, can change a very stressed-out person trying to control all the goings-on in their life to a person whose life is simply under control.

Time given to meditation and relaxation is a letting-go of the unimportant things outside ourselves and keeping close to our heart the essentials of life. In this way we gain control of our life and see clearly our priorities, fully aware of obligations and quietly enjoying carrying them out.

TIP TO GO:
Write a 'Things I'd love to do' list.

CAN'T

'I can't' seems to be a phrase that constantly surfaces throughout our life. We may become so used to hearing 'I can't do that' or 'I can't change' or any number of situations where 'I can't' constantly crops up, that we actually believe it to be true. In fact, it may just be a cover-up phrase for feeling silly when trying something new, taking a risk of some sort or attempting to get out of a rut.

You may like to give up smoking, give up unnecessary medication, or get involved in a new enterprise. Before you even try, there before you every time you think about it is a barrage of 'I can't's.

What you don't realise is the reason you can't is because you perhaps haven't even made an attempt, or if you have, haven't practised enough. To become good at anything takes time, effort and dedication. If you want something enough and are prepared to pay the price, it will be yours. So the 'I can't's are negatives to be put out of your life. For every 'I can't', you need to utter a positive 'I can'. 'Of course I can and I will!'

The positive statement 'I can' fills you with ideas how to bring about what you want. It's more than just saying 'I can'. It supplies you with the energy to experiment. It takes you on a journey of exploration, to places you've never been before. It builds your self esteem and confidence to a point where turning back would mean settling for second best; and who wants that?

TIP TO GO:
Take a dive into the adventurous side of your nature.

CHALLENGES

It's so healthy to have a challenge in your life. You may not see it this way when you have it, but challenges make you strong and more able to cope with future problems. Challenges build up your spiritual immune system.

No matter what type of challenge it is, if seen in the right light, it will bring you an untold amount of spiritual riches, riches that God has stored up for you, only to be released when you see the positive side of the challenge.

Welcome every challenge that comes your way - worries of all shapes and sizes, relationship problems, physical pains and aches. They all manifest as some form of weakness which you have to face every single day. Take out your positive face, put it on and rise to each challenge as it comes into your space.

TIP TO GO:
Always welcome a challenge, whatever it is. Then your mind is open to solutions. If you're negative, you close yourself off, thereby blocking any good ideas you might have about how to handle the situation.

CHANGE

Change can be traumatic, but it has to be done sometimes. When change takes place, life is disturbed, but change can be hugely positive. It gives you a different perspective, helps you see yourself and your situation in an entirely new light.

Change can help your life go in the direction you want. You may feel these changes to be good, but you've no way of knowing for sure. You just have to go on faith.

Changes can help you have more confidence in yourself, in your higher nature. During the 'change' period, a lot of different emotions may surface, such as annoyance, irritation, hurt, anger.

Keep an eye on your goal. Ignore negative feelings and thoughts. Stay focused and continue to make efforts. You will reap great benefits.

TIP TO GO:
Change your normal routine.
Dress differently.

CREATING THE WORLD WE WANT

It begins with me and you. But, more specifically, I am the one responsible for the way the world is, or at least the way my world is.

Living in the moment and enjoying it fully; loving our neighbour, God, and doing meaningful work; have we not then a good chance to create a world where love reigns supreme?

Many songwriters claim that 'Love is all you need', and poets declare 'Give me love and I can court the whole world'. One's contribution to a loving world can be manifold. A kind look. A stare averted. An encouraging word. A helping hand. Allowable independence.

The transforming power of love is unique and the more love is present in our hearts, and therefore in the world, the more we create exactly the world we want.

TIP TO GO:
Delve into the depths of yourself for more love.
Argument and criticism destroy love.

TIMES OF DISTRESS

How can we create a stronghold against the negative elements that sometimes enter our lives?

We need firstly to be aware of who our enemy is. Sometimes, our worst enemy can be ourself and, without realising it, we give in and cause ourself an untold amount of suffering. Every person has several weak points, but our strength comes from knowing where they are, when they are active and what to do when we are in a state of weakness. That may be the time to call on God, to ask Him to help us out, to give Him the chance to show us that He loves us.

His help can come in many different ways. Perhaps just talking to a friend, reading an inspiring book or watching a funny movie.

TIP TO GO:
Be gentle with yourself when you are weak.
Do something creative you really enjoy.

PASSING THROUGH

Even though we are nearly always with other people, we are essentially on our own. No matter who we are with, or how many, we are still on our own. We came into the world on our own and we leave it on our own.

A great place to be on your own and, at the same time, be with others is when you go to church. Just you and God all alone, surrounded by people, yes, but not directly communicating with anyone. And, at the same time, communicating with God if you choose.

Realising you are on your own in the world can be a great strength and comfort at times. Because the reality is you are just passing through, going from one place to another, and, although you are alone, you influence those around you and take them with you on your journey, no matter what direction you take.

TIP TO GO:
See the good.
Hear the good.
Speak the good.

'ANGELS'

Saint Columcille loved the city of Derry because, he said, 'It is full of white angels from one end to the other'. Our acquaintance with angles usually starts when we are young, when we're told we have a Guardian Angel, someone who looks after and protects us in time of trouble or danger. Angels, of course, are not just confined to Derry, but are to be found all over the world, in unusual places and under extraordinary circumstances. Perhaps all we have to do is to ask for help and they will come.

Several years ago, some friends and I went on a faith-mission to Denmark. Our plan was to beg for food and hitchhike in three's. 'You'll never get anywhere with three', was the cry of parents and friends. 'It's hard enough to give a lift to two. But THREE, never!'. As it was a faith-mission, we relished the challenge and took as our mission statement 'Where there are two or more gathered in My Name, there I am in the midst of them'. What an amazing journey! We met 'Angels' at every turn.

We sailed from Dun Laoghaire to Holyhead. From there, lifts were supplied all the way to Dover, where we crossed to Belgium. A thumb was hardly out when we were offered another lift from a man who didn't speak any English at all. We tried to explain where we wanted to go; he just smiled. It was late when we reached the next town, where he lived, so he offered us a floor for the night. He had one bedroom and a kitchen. The bedroom had a double bed which he offered us, but we declined and hauled out our sleeping bags, sleeping on the floor on both sides of his bed. We called him 'our angel'. We knew nothing about him. What an unusual situation. We laughed ourselves to sleep.

When he got up, next morning, he went straight out without even looking in our direction. 20 minutes later, he returned with a whole assortment of freshly baked bread. He brewed us coffee and we tried our very best to communicate with our little French. Breakfast over, he brought us to the highway where we waved goodbye to our Belgian 'angel'.

Our next lift was a gentleman returning to Holland, having left his son at boarding school. He brought us to a fancy restaurant, where we were wined and dined. His reason - he felt so lonely after leaving his son to school.

Our Dutch 'angel' left us off on the German border, where we met up with a German couple returning home from Disneyland with their kids. We squashed into the car with their kids and were treated to a hot bath, dinner and a room for the night.

Our German 'angels' left us to the nearest highway. Eventually, we made it to Denmark, taking eight days in all. Although we all have a Guardian Angel, there are plenty of other 'angels' going around at the same time. It bodes well for the European community when the hand of friendship is extended to less fortunate neighbours. When the weakest link is taken care of, the chains that are formed can be very strong.

TIP TO GO:
Listen to your inner voice and follow your heart. Faith matures in darkness.

HEALING

Healing takes place in an environment of peace, calm and tranquillity. It is not necessarily a place, but an environment you create within yourself.

A space or a haven, where you can go and recreate your spirit, take charge of yourself and everything that happens in your life. This space belongs only to you.

Your essential space is surrounded by love for yourself, love for truth and love for freedom.

TIP TO GO:
Lay aside the past, all of the past.
Forgive and move on.

MEDITATION

How wonderful to relax and be still. Meditation is a time set aside for complete silence, bringing you a little closer to health in mind, body and spirit. To meditate is always a healing experience.

Set aside some time every day to meditate. To meditate is coming face to face with yourself, your neighbour and God. In this silent time, in the presence of God, decisions are made and carried out. You are becoming a whole person.

Before you enter your quiet space, turn off all phones. This is your special time. No deadlines. No interruptions. Just peaceful meditation.

Enter your quiet space, peacefully.

TIP TO GO:
Never miss your special time for meditation.

NEW YORK

I looked forward to my first visit to New York with enthusiasm. As the taxi stopped outside our hotel, I had to crane my neck to gaze awe-struck at the skyscraper we had just booked into. I was appalled. How could I have made such a mistake? Our room was on the 35th floor. I was faint at the thought of it. Why? I have a phobia about elevators, enclosed spaces and being any higher than the third floor.

Dog-tired and 2 a.m. in the morning helped me to grit my teeth, close my eyes and hold on tightly to my friend till we got to our room – a magnificent view of New York City. Fabulous!

Our reason for booking this particular hotel was we had been looking forward to swimming every day (one whole floor is a pool and gym), but I was haunted by my fear. Even though we enjoyed the city sights, the fear was still there as we returned to our hotel. I enquired if we could have a room closer to the ground floor, but there were no vacancies below us. Out of my mind with fear, I felt I couldn't spend another night in the hotel. Here we were at the height of the tourist season looking for another hotel in downtown Manhattan, one that would suit our budget!

We found one on 51st street, within walking distance of most places of interest. The only problem with the new place was my friend couldn't sleep because of street-noise; we changed to a quieter room. Peace at last.

It was such an interesting experience overall. Our friendship grew. I had faced my fears in a new way, accepted what I wasn't able for, forgave myself and moved on.

Life is not always feeling the fear and doing it anyway.

TIP TO GO:
Treasure whatever weakness you have.
See all the positive possibilities of weakness.

BE IN THE NOW

Be in the now. Sometimes we think: 'I'd love to say something intelligent in a certain situation. I'd love to be a genius at something.' These are thoughts that sometimes go through our heads.

You are unique, now. You are in the moment, now. By living in the moment, by loving in the moment, you are giving more glory to God than if you said and did great things.

It is powerful to be yourself. Your wonderful, beautiful, intelligent self. Now. You make choices that are good. Well done! You work at what you love. Congratulations! There are areas to improve. Be grateful for your insight!

The Present Moment is brimming over with wondrous things to be discovered. Unearth all your treasures. Now!

TIP TO GO:
Enjoy every moment.
Don't worry about the future
Be creative now.

OPPORTUNITIES

Opportunities present themselves all the time, provided we are free, unfettered and not tied down by petty strings of stubbornness, grumbling or negative expressions.

Loving is a full time job. We must scout for beauty at all times. Be on the lookout. Like a photographer always watching for that elusive picture, let us be just as diligent to see beauty, inhale it when we do catch a glimpse, enjoy it, let it go and continue our search for more and more.

Beauty is the daily food of love. If we neglect our daily food, what will happen to us? Who knows? One thing's for sure, you can light up your life with love. Opportunities are there for the taking!

TIP TO GO:
To the business man, every situation is a chance to earn an extra penny.
To the person who wants to love God, every situation is an opportunity for more love.

RESPONDING TO INSPIRATIONS

Responding to inspirations can be the beginning of leading an exciting and fulfilling life. Being tuned into the tiny whispers that come throughout your day can make your day very interesting and spiritually uplifting.

Inspirations can be varied: I read about a woman who wanted to skydive, even though she had MS (Multiple Sclerosis). When she landed, she found that her MS was gone! What an amazing outcome from following an inspiration.

Don't waste time moaning about your life. Take time out to enjoy yourself… Eat a more healthful diet. Contact an old friend. Visit an elderly neighbour. Learn a language. Take a Balloon Ride or try a Bungee Jump. Numerous inspirations are lost forever because they are ignored. Whereas a response to an inspiration can truly make someone's day, as well as enriching yourself and the world around you.

TIP TO GO:
Tune in to all your whispers.

'SMALL'

Being 'small' is such an attractive state when you are actually 'small', but such a stumbling block when you're not. I suppose another name for 'small' is being humble. Pride can make us irritated with those who are 'small', who get in the way when we want something done. We don't realise that happiness is found in loving the way others are, loving the way we are, and then aspiring to something new and higher.

Being honest, agreeable and loveable takes time and effort. But that's what makes life interesting: having the courage to discipline yourself so that you can live in your community, relationship or family. Peacefully.

The 'small' always get what they want, be it from parents, God or friends. It's hard to resist the charm and attractiveness of one who is 'small'. The person who knows and loves who they are loves their state of weakness, yet doesn't run from it. They admit weakness and go towards it with open arms. Yes, there is a lot to learn from being 'small', just being who you are without having to be afraid; without having to run, grumble, complain or justify yourself; just moving forward with hope, courage and love.

To be 'small' is to be what God wants you to be. To do what God wants you to do. To be where God wants you to be. As it says in the psalms, 'God cannot resist the prayer of the humble.'

TIP TO GO:
Explore all the possibilities of being 'small'.
Enjoy your discoveries.

WHAT WOULD WE DO?

If everything around us, excluding the human race, was reduced to dust for 12 hours, what would we do? What would be left?

We couldn't go to work because we would have no transport. No place to work. No shops to buy anything. No food, no drink; but above all, no distractions. Our only occupation for those 12 hours would be spent in the presence of other human beings, our nearest family and friends perhaps. In other words, our neighbours.

Suddenly, we would be aware of the importance of these people we so often forget about. The importance of communication, sharing, comforting and encouraging. We might discover that the source of happiness and peace lies in being there for one another.

We might also become aware that God has put us here to love Him and to love each other, and, as long as we have those two loves firmly established in our heart and reap the beauty thereof, the whole earth can crumble.

TIP TO GO:
Lend a helping hand. Always.

'WIMP'

'Wimp' is a word that seems to be used a lot nowadays. What does the word imply? It means a person who is weak, not strong; a person who doesn't want to do what is 'required' of them. In other words, a wimp could be a person of courage - what you see is what you get.

A wimp could be a person who doesn't hide their weakness in any way, and so may be victimised by the 'stronger' members of society. And it may also be that the wimp is a really content person, living their own life in their own happy way, who in no way lines up to conventional ways of doing things; a person who does not tow the party line, but marches to their own drum.

In short, a wimp may be hero!

TIP TO GO:
Follow your inner voice at all times. It will bring you an untold amount of happiness and, most of all, peace.

YOU ARE A UNIQUE PERSON

You are a unique person. The discovery of your own uniqueness is found when you begin to love exactly who you are. You are the only one of your kind. An original.

Loving who you are sets the unique person inside you free. You need to love yourself a lot, because at every moment you have the capability of taking yourself down with self-criticism and fault-finding. If this is the case, it's time to stop and take a look at what you are doing to your self-esteem, confidence and dignity as a human being.

Yes, we all have a dark side and facing this makes it possible to transform it into something good. Each weakness we have can become a great strength. We make that transition through love.

Through love comes the discovery of your unique potential. Love the things that make you unique - your looks, your gifts and talents, your thoughts and ideas, everything that makes up the unique you.

Discovering and respecting your own uniqueness causes you to thoroughly respect the dignity and uniqueness of others.

TIP TO GO:
Be extremely patient with yourself.
Set your mind to change what needs to be changed.
Then it will effortlessly take place.

IN EVERY PROBLEM THERE'S A GIFT

This is one popular saying I like a lot. I suppose because it seems to be true, nearly all the time.

We have a choice when we are faced with a problem: to moan about it, or see the gift behind it. I'm sure there are hundreds of examples out there of problems that turned out to be the best things that ever happened. But those success stories belong to other people. The important thing is to have your own. To change your own problems into gifts. To come up with a positive solution every time something turns sour on you. It could be a failed friendship, being let go from your job, falling and hurting yourself, losing your money, missing your plane, not finding your car in the parking lot. There are any number of problems to be transformed into gifts and they are special to you.

Your choice makes the whole difference. It's a wonderful discipline to take on board not to leave a situation alone until you come up with a positive solution or way of dealing with it. I suppose it's a form of wisdom that requires practice. It's about becoming adaptable, even in extraordinary circumstances. And that's what makes the ordinary person into a hero, even if it's only a hero in your own eyes. Because how you feel about yourself is really important. And you are affected by every thought you have about yourself and your problems.

When you choose to change a problem into a gift, your mind expands, thereby allowing a unique set of completely positive thoughts to enter your consciousness. The negative thoughts just fade into the background. You are now well on your way to a very happy solution.

TIP TO GO:
Be 100% optimistic.
When you change the way you think, you change your outward circumstances.

PHILOMENA

It was a warm March afternoon when my mother came home with the new baby. I had a new sister! I couldn't wait to see her. When I looked in at the warm cosy bundle, I immediately knew something was different. She didn't have the normal looks of a new baby. I remember running down to my friend's house to tell her the news – 'Our baby is handicapped!' I'm not sure they were the words I used, but she understood. I was a kid at the time and had no awareness of the pain of this event. It was many years later my mother told me the heart-breaking story of how she had contracted German measles and knew already that my sister could have one of many conditions. She had to go through that trauma and, on top of that, she had another trauma: my father initially found it difficult to look at his new daughter - a child with Down Syndrome.

Philomena was an extremely quiet baby, never cried much, never moved much either, even though the rest of the family, all six of us, played with her endlessly. Then something extraordinary happened. My eldest sister came back from holidays in Spain and in her possession she had an LP (long playing vinyl record) of Flamenco music. The first moment that Philomena heard the music she suddenly took on a new life. She was hopping up and down in her pram, smiling and laughing. The bonds were broken and everyone in the family was delighted. Consequently, Flamenco music blared out from the record player morning, noon and night.

Philomena was a new person. She grew up with a passion for music. Then, Michael Jackson became the number one person in her life. She loved everything about him. How he sang, how he danced. She had his CDs, DVDs, went to his concerts, carried pictures of him everywhere. She became his number one fan.

She worked at St. Michael's House in Ballymun, Dublin with other Down Syndrome people. She loved being with her friends and wouldn't miss a day's work, even when she was sick.

Probably thanks to Michael Jackson, she had a passion for playing the drums. My parents bought her a drum kit. She took drumming lessons and loved to entertain with her drum flourishes.

She was in love with life and with people. It didn't matter who they were. Strangers, foreigners, black or white - all were greeted and, if at all possible, hugged and appreciated.

She was the darling of the family. She was so funny. She inherited my father's sense of humour and he brought her with him everywhere. They worked closely together and she always made him a great cup of tea. She increased her comedy antics, maybe because her favourite TV programmes were comedy shows. She could do a superb imitation of them all – Tommy Cooper, Les Dawson, the Two Ronnies,

Morecambe and Wise.

She had an amazing memory and could speak greetings in Danish, French and Irish, and always knew the correct time and place for them.

Her favourite night was dance night where she met her friends and they danced the night away to their favourite pop stars.

She entered the Special Olympics and won a bunch of medals for all sorts of sports - long jump, swimming, snooker, to mention but a few. When visitors came to the house, out came the medals!

After my father died, she was a great consolation to my mother. As everyone had left home, Philomena was there to console and even make my mother laugh at all the silly antics she would get up to.

Philomena lived in care for four years, having lived at home for fifty. In the last few years of her life she developed Alzheimer's disease and was bedridden. She used to call me all sorts of names, never my own. But one thing she hadn't forgotten was how to give you a huge bear hug. She died in October 2012.

When she was brought into the crematorium in Glasnevin cemetery, the man in charge asked us what music we would like played for her. We mentioned that she loved Michael Jackson, and then forgot about it as they played a prayerful hymn for the introduction. Then, as the curtains slowly closed, so that you could see the coffin no more, Michael Jackson's voice rang out with 'You are not alone'. There was not a dry eye in the place. It was amazingly beautiful and appropriate too.

What a wonderful life she lived! A life where she spread an endless amount of joy and love. By now, she has more than likely met the love of her life, Michael Jackson, and they have danced together among the stars and maybe even done the moonwalk!

PROGRAMMES BY GABRIELLE KIRBY

CDs
Let's Relax
Super Relaxation
Meditation
Thoughts to Power Your Day
Thoughts to Power Your Life
Heal Your Self
Bereavement
Respond to Your Heart and Be Who You Are
Glendalough – A Celtic Journey
The Power of the Present Moment
Peaceful Meditation

DVDs
Let's Relax
Peaceful Meditation
Glendalough – A Mystical Journey
Gabrielle's Journey
Train Games
In the Same Boat
Business Partners

BOOKS
The Secret's Inside
You Can Heal Your Self, I Did
New Reflections

www.gabriellekirby.com

HEALTHY HOLIDAY RETREATS

Gabrielle runs Healthy Holiday Retreats in sunny climates such as Spain, Greece, Italy and the Canary Islands.

They are usually for 7 days. The cuisine is Gourmet Raw Food, and the programme also includes Guided Meditation, Health Presentations, Awareness Walks, Light Exercise, an Entertaining Night Out, as well as plenty of free time to enjoy the beach and the surrounding area.

Please see **www.gabriellekirby.com** for details.

ALIVE

The Irish Living Foods Association, of which Gabrielle is an active organiser, holds monthly meetings at the SOL Health Centre in Wicklow Town, Ireland.

The event features a speaker who specialises in a specific area of health and who gives a presentation on effective ways to live a more healthy life. After the presentation comes a Raw Food Preparation Demonstration. This is followed by a Raw Food Buffet.

www.irishlivingfoods.com